Nelson English

Beginning Non-fiction Skills

RED
LEVEL

John Jackman **Wendy Wren**

Holidays unit 1

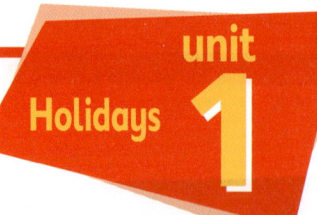

On the Beach

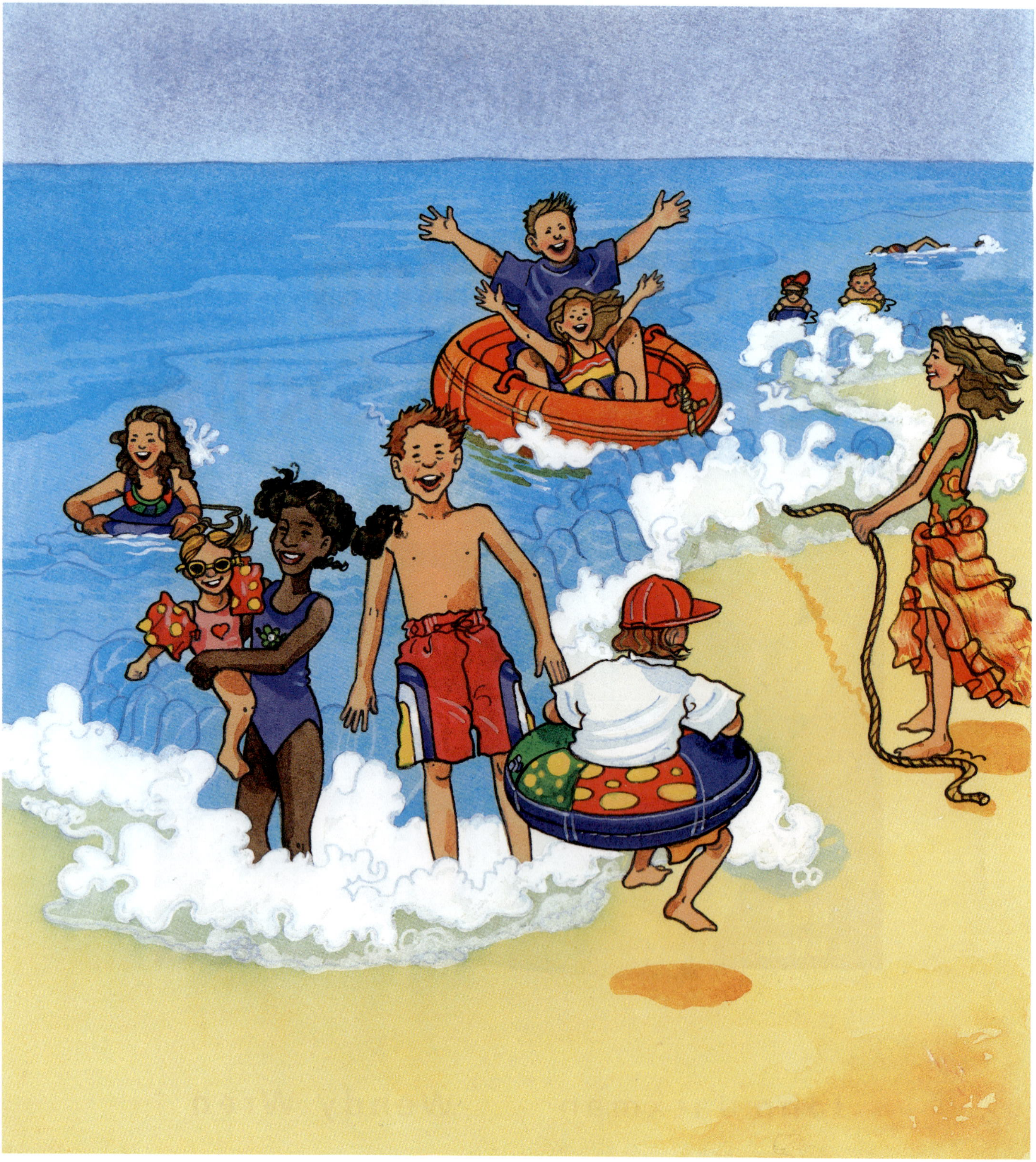

The waves are big.

The children make a sandcastle.

SOFT ICE CREAM

99

The children like ice-cream.

It is hot in the sun.

unit **2**

Party Time

hat

drink

cake

bun

jelly

jug

cup

dog

Food unit 3

How to make Ice-lollies

You will need:
jug
fruit squash
water
ice-lolly mould
lolly sticks

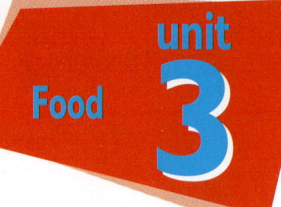

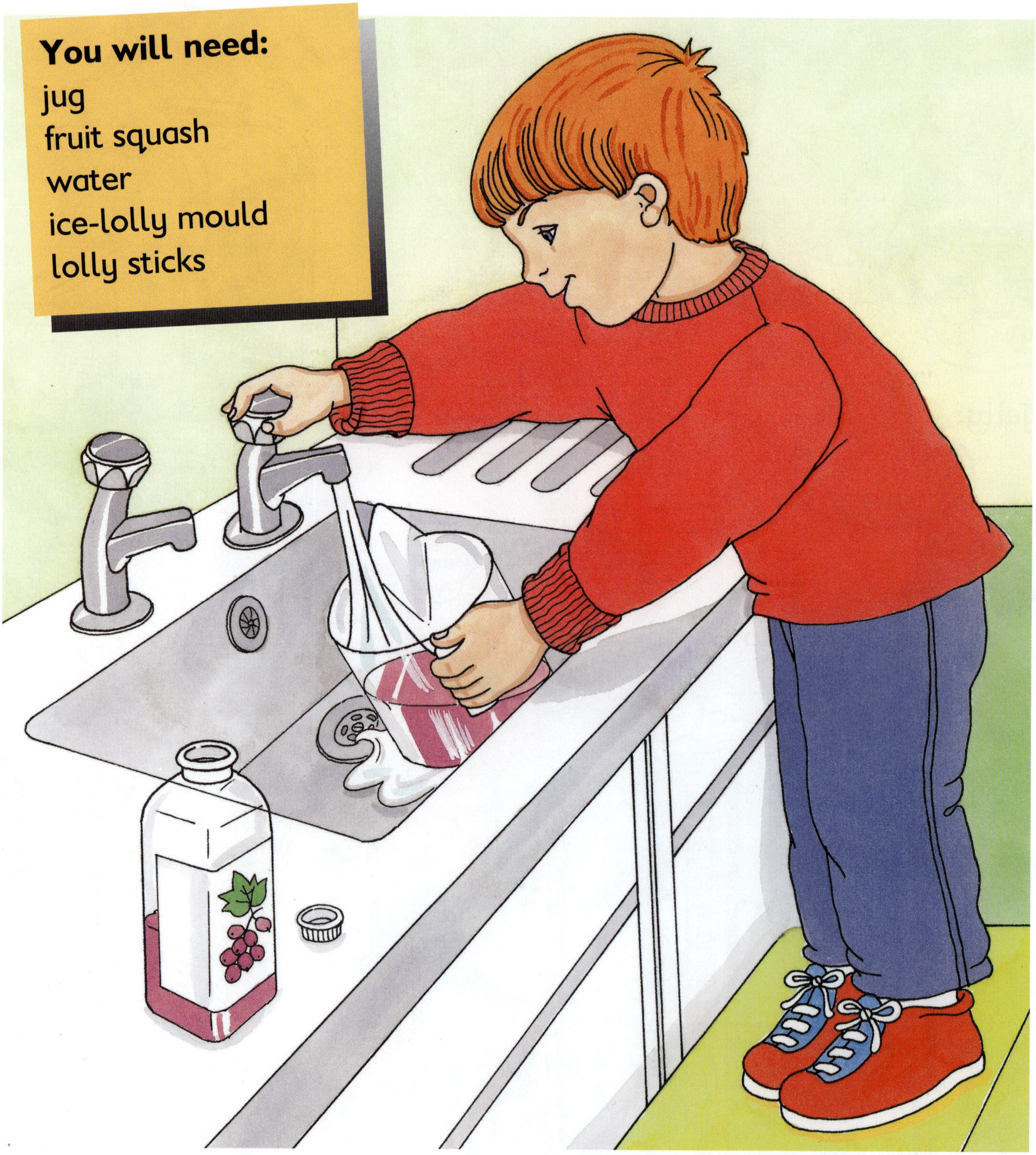

1 Mix the fruit squash with water in the jug.

2 Pour it into the ice-lolly mould.

3 Put in the lolly sticks.

4 Put the ice-lolly mould into the freezer.

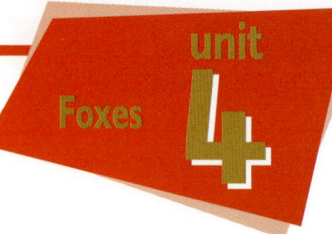

All about Foxes

This is the front cover of a book about foxes.

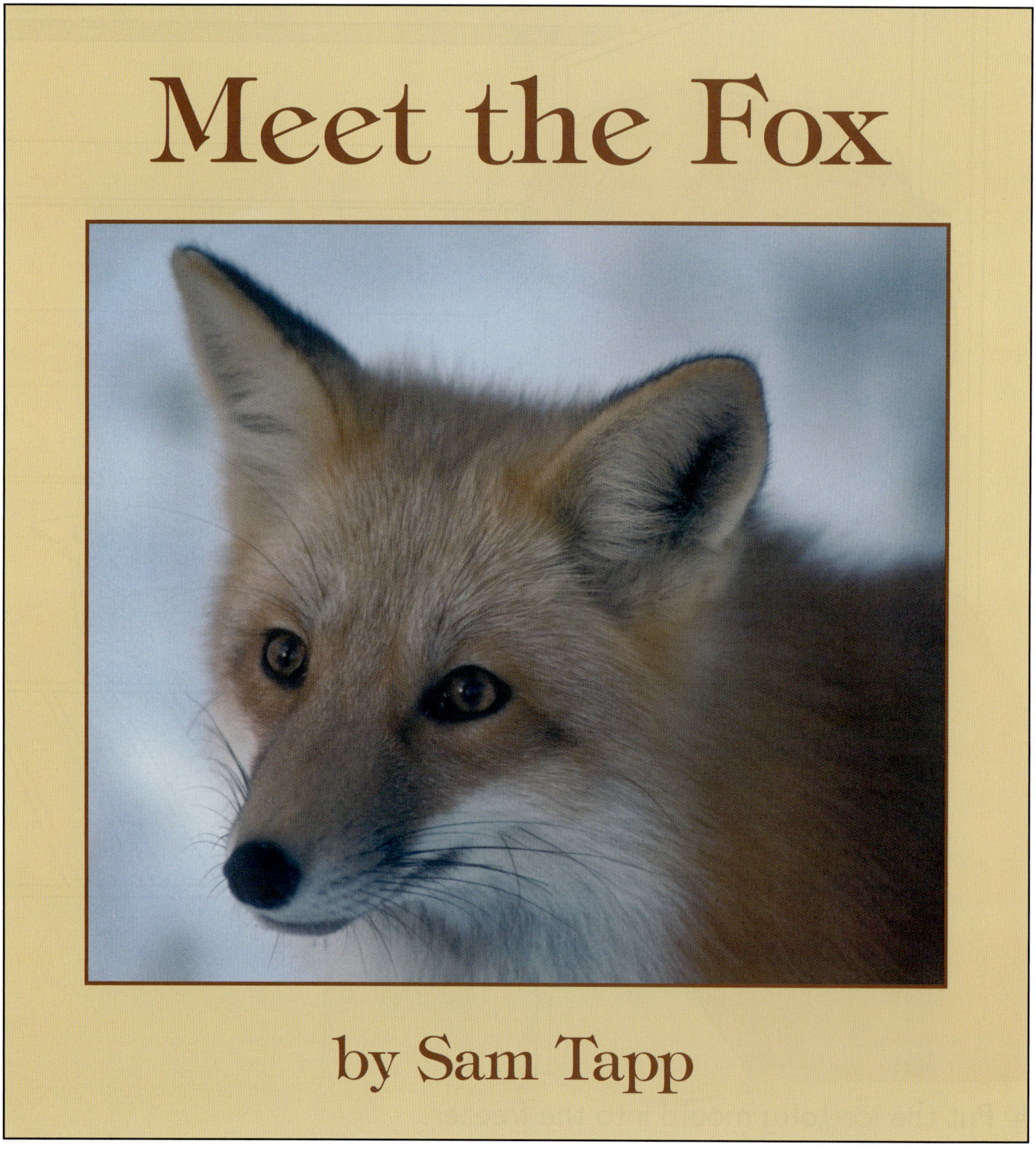

Meet the Fox

by Sam Tapp

This is the back cover of the book about foxes.

This book tells you about foxes.

- It tells you what they look like.
- It tells you where they live.
- It tells you what they eat.

If you want to learn about foxes,
read this book!

Here are some pages from the book about foxes.

Where do foxes live?

Many foxes live in the countryside.

4

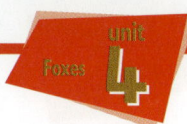

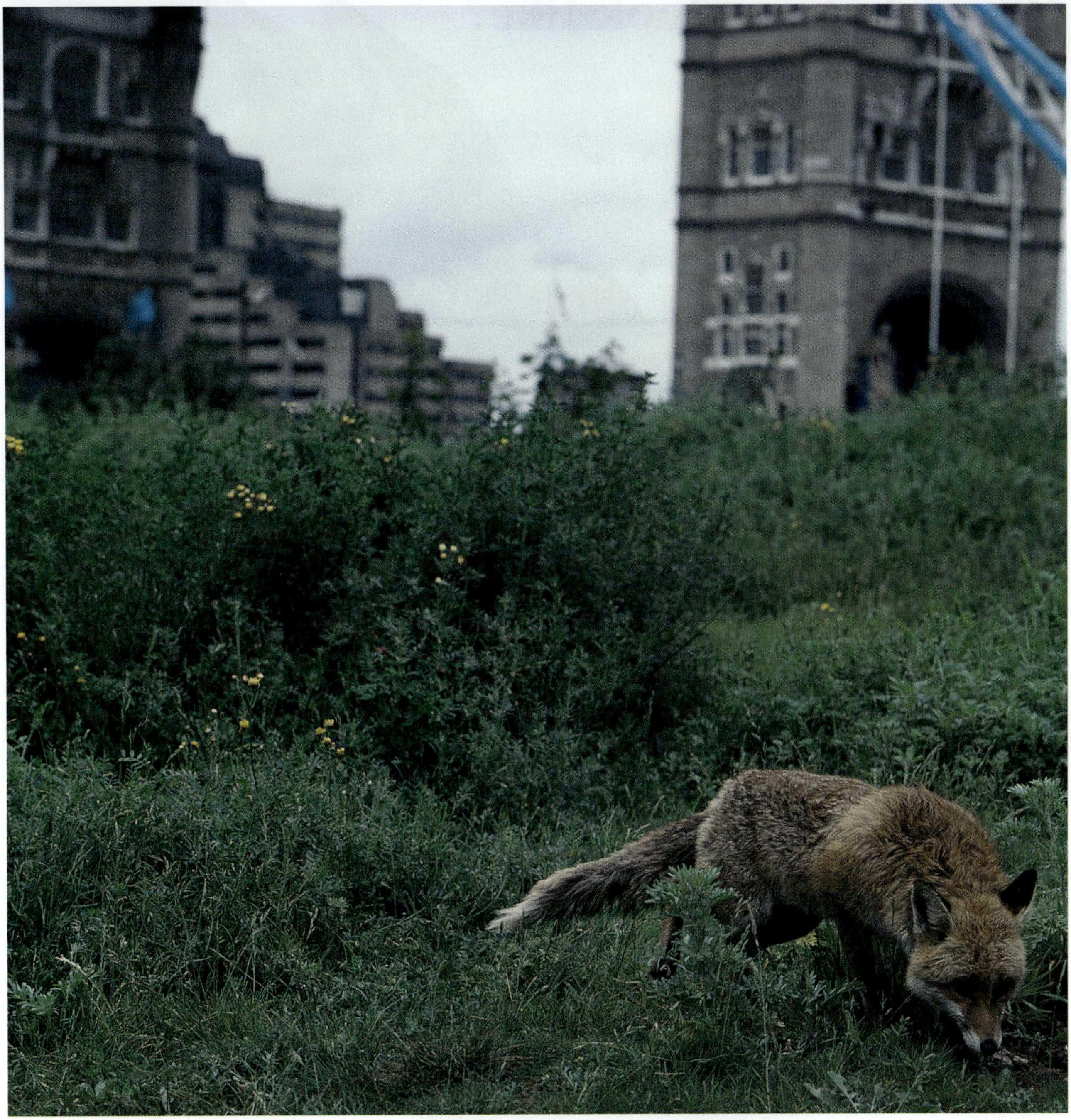

Lots of foxes now live in towns and cities.

5

What do foxes look like?

reddish-brown fur

pointed nose

whiskers

white patches

bushy tail

6

What do foxes eat?

Foxes are hunters.

They hunt small animals, birds and insects.

Foxes sometimes eat fruit.

7

Beans

unit 5

Growing Beans

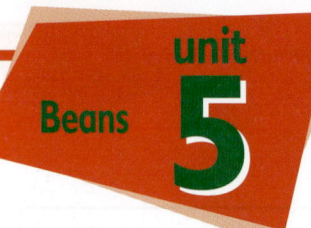

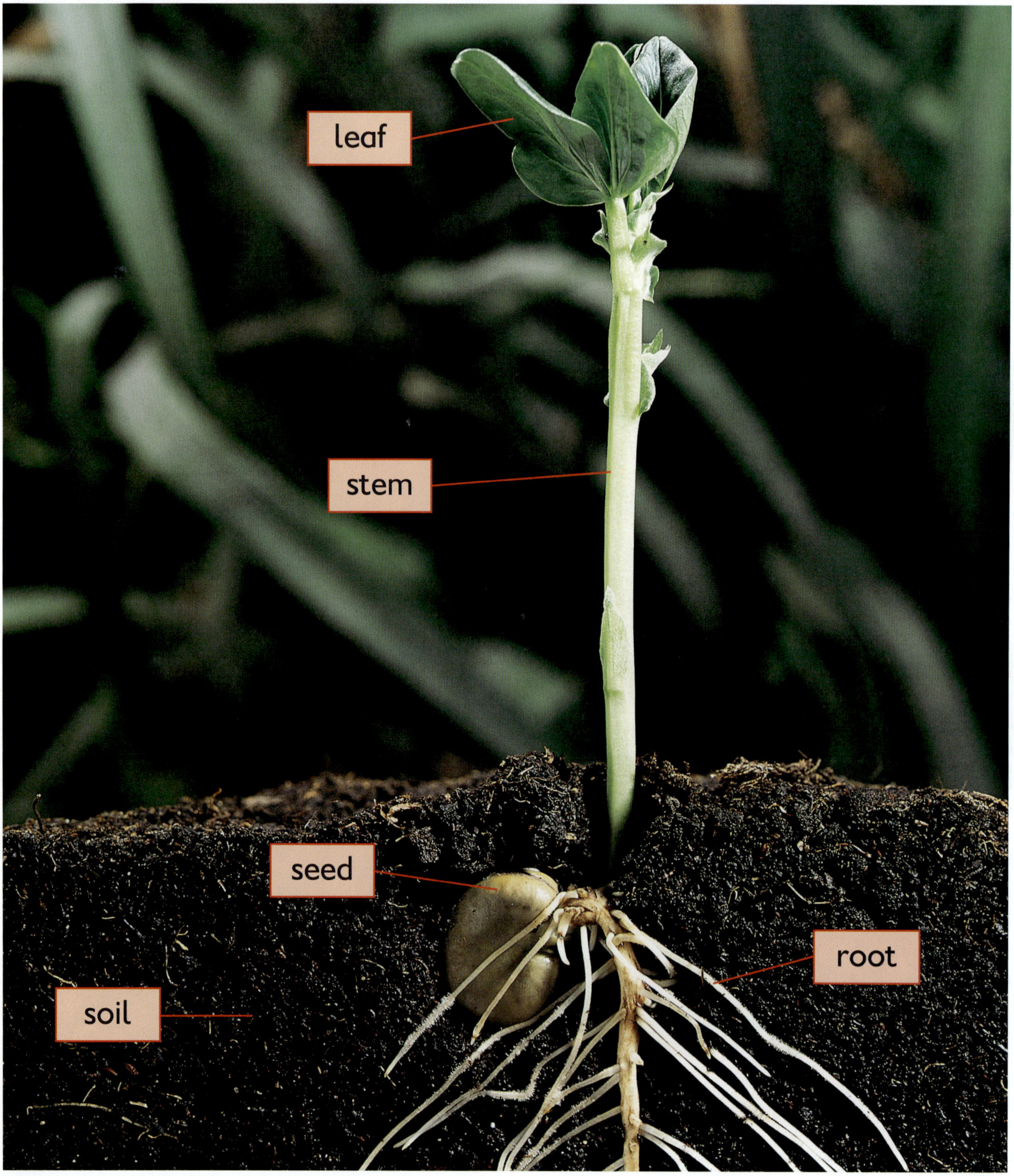
leaf
stem
seed
root
soil

stem

flower

bean

leaf

Toys

A **dictionary** is a list of words and their meanings.

The words are in **alphabetical order**.

Here is part of a dictionary about toys.

ball

A round, bouncy toy you can throw, kick and catch.

doll

A toy that looks like a baby or a child.

kite

A toy that flies in the air on the end of a long string.

skipping-rope

A rope that you swing and jump over.

teddy bear

A cuddly toy that looks like a bear.

Here is the alphabet.

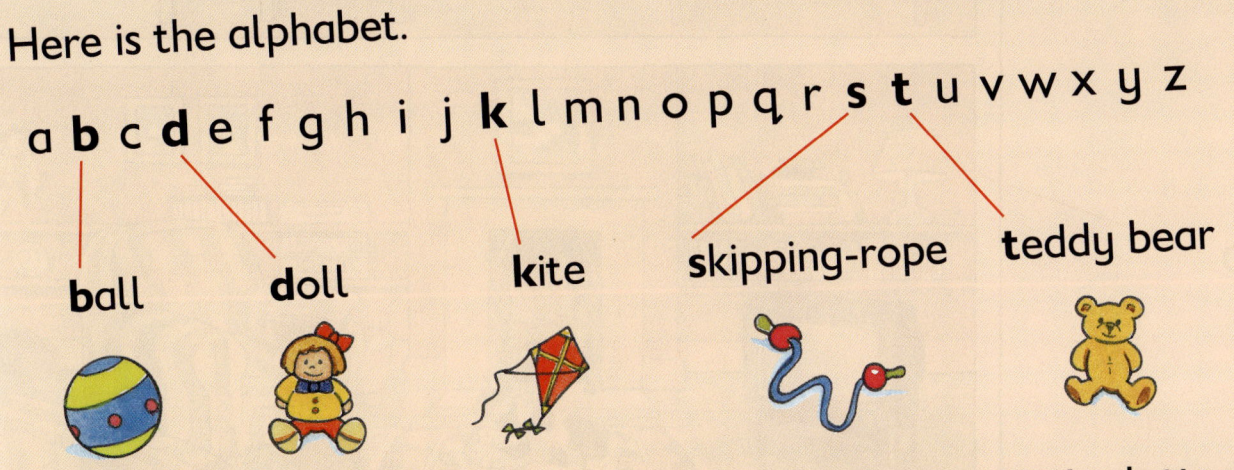

a **b** c **d** e f g h i j **k** l m n o p q r **s** **t** u v w x y z

ball   **d**oll   **k**ite   **s**kipping-rope   **t**eddy bear

The words in the dictionary are in the same order as the letters in the alphabet.

Homes **unit 7**

Inside a House

door

cot

lamp

chair

bedroom

living-room

22

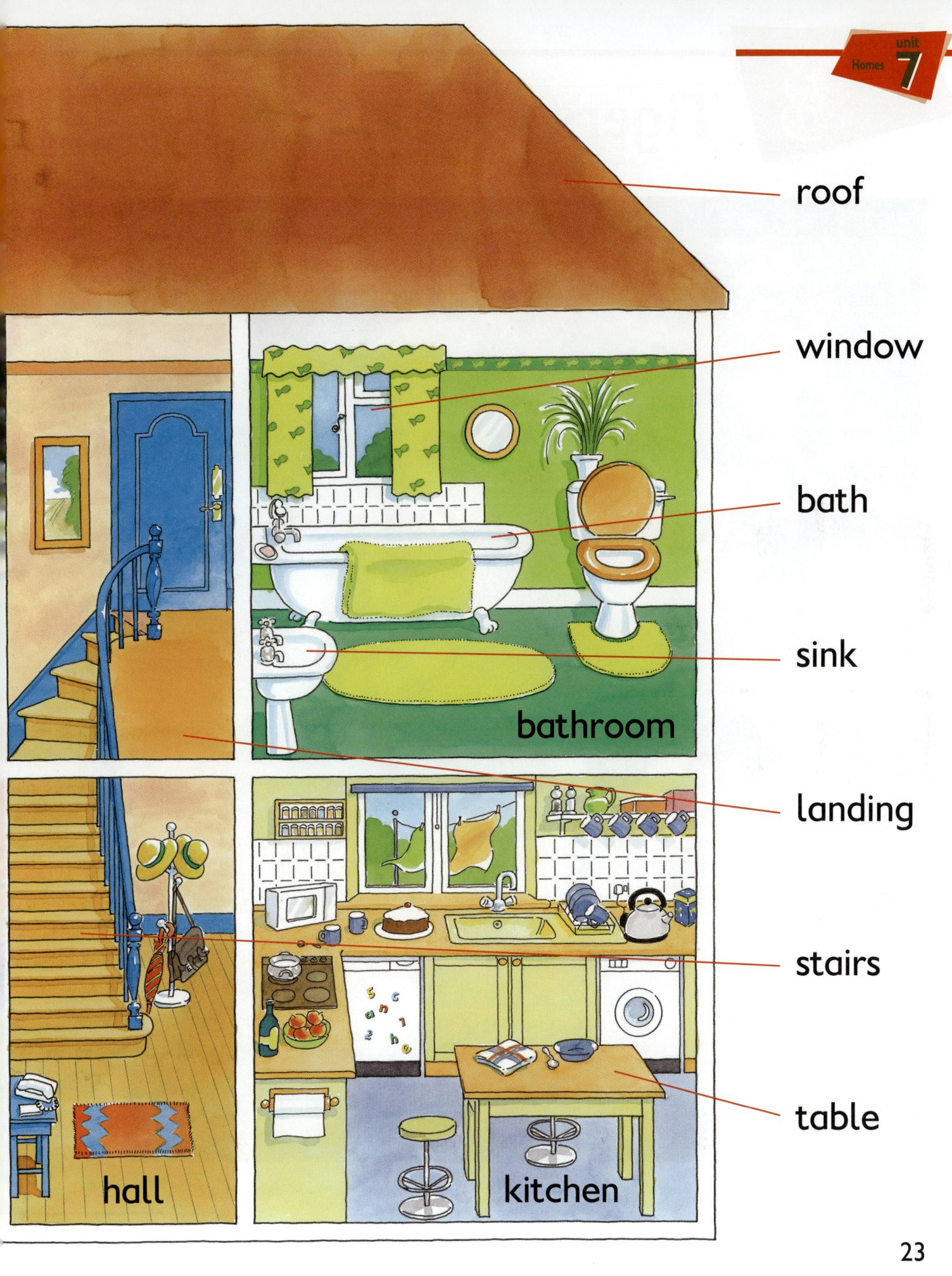

roof

window

bath

sink

bathroom

landing

stairs

table

hall

kitchen

23

unit
Tigers 8

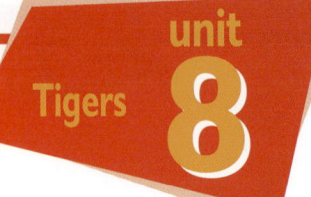

Tigers

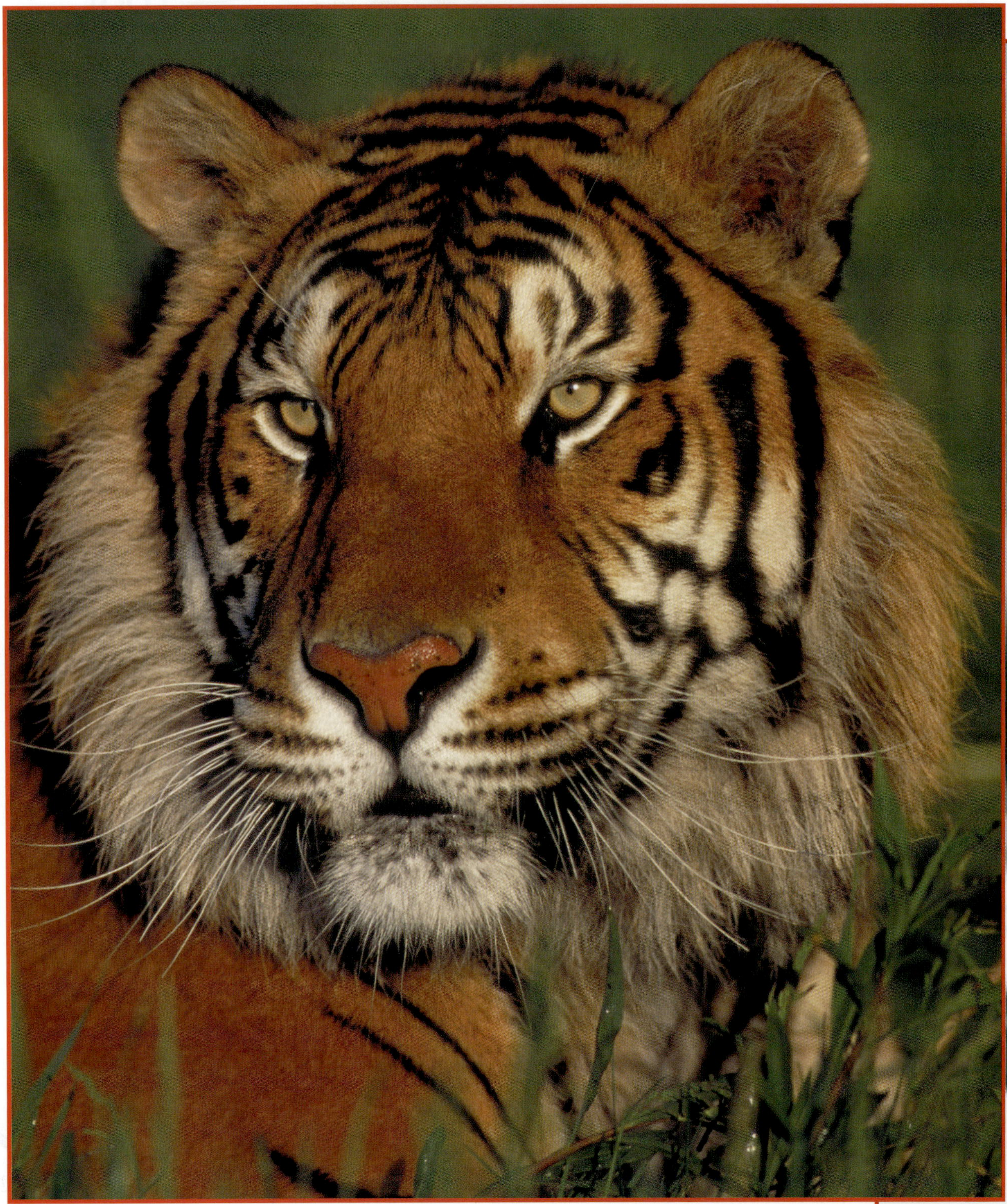

Tigers are big cats.

Most tigers live in hot places such as India.
Some tigers live in cold places such as Siberia.

A tigress can give birth to as many as seven cubs.

Usually only two or three survive.

The cubs spend eight weeks in the den, feeding on their mother's milk.

Fact File

What tigers look like

Most tigers have orange fur with black stripes.

Some tigers have paler fur and fewer stripes.

Male tigers are bigger than female tigers.

How tigers live

Tigers do not live in families or groups.

Tigers live and hunt on their own.

What tigers eat

Tigers hunt at night.

Tigers catch deer and wild pigs.

Tigers will eat most small animals.

How tigers move

Tigers are not fast runners.

Tigers creep up on an animal and pounce.

Tigers can swim.

Growing up

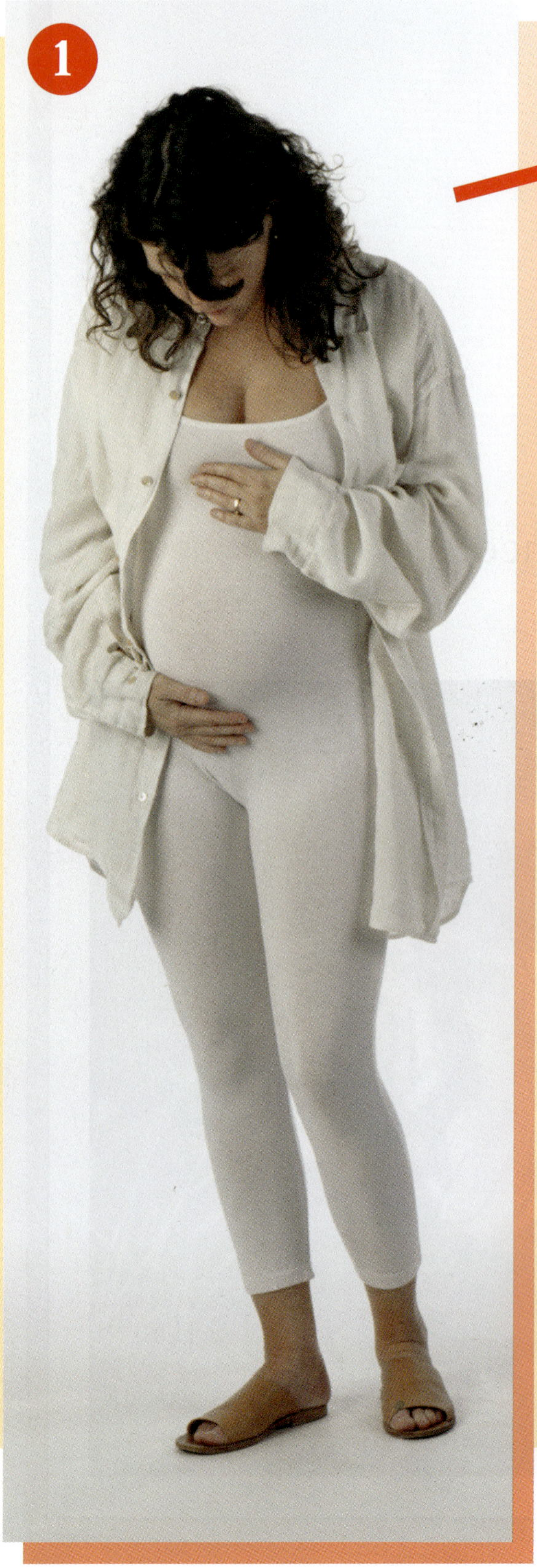

1

2

3

7

8

q